Coffee and Bible

30 Days of Scripture and Inspiration to Nourish Your Spirit

Meagan Trayler

Copyright 2018, 2022 Meagan Trayler - All rights reserved.

In no way is it legal to reproduce, duplicate, or transmit any part of this document in either electronic means or in printed format. All rights reserved.

A note to the reader-

The information provided in this document is not intended to diagnose, treat, or otherwise substitute professional care. The information provided here is to be used at the reader's discretion only. The author is not liable for any use or misuse of this work. If proper assistance is required a professional should be sought.

Table of Contents

Introduction 5
Day 1 Have a Vision 6
Day 2 Lead Your Heart 9
Day 3 Body Image 11
Day 4 Be Still and Know 13
Day 5 Forgiveness 15
Day 6 Life-Giving Tongue 17
Day 7 Fear 19
Day 8 Doubt 21
Day 9 Be A Life-Giver 23
Day 10 Pursuing Excellence 25
Day 11 Embrace Your Uniqueness 28
Day 12 Nurturing Relationships 30
Day 13 Your Purpose for Dating 32
Day 14 You're Not Alone 34
Day 15 You Are Enough 36
Day 16 Be Of Use 38
Day 17 Choosing Joy 41
Day 18 Deepest Cuts 43

Day 19	The Comparison Trap	45
Day 20	Do Him Good	47
Day 21	Self-Talk	49
Day 22	Step Outside the Drama	51
Day 23	Made on Purpose	53
Day 24	Acknowledge Him	55
Day 25	It's a Heart Issue	57
Day 26	Be a Leader	59
Day 27	Feelings-Tricky Little Things	61
Day 28	Respect is a Reflection of You	64
Day 29	What Are You Wearing?	66
Day 30	Be Your Whole You	68
Author's Note		70
Want More?		71

Introduction

This devotional was born out of my childhood. Every morning I would go downstairs to find my Mom sitting somewhere with a cup of coffee and an open Bible. Her coffee would be lukewarm and her mind filled with Godly things. It was her habit. I adopted it, and now it's mine. In my subconscious, Coffee and Bible has become less a memory and more an association. They just go together.

I hope the words in this book, specifically the scriptures, speak to you. May you know the love of God, so you will be filled to the measure of all the fullness of Him (Ephesians 3:19).

Meagan Trayler

Day 1

Have a Vision

We go through our days at breakneck speed sometimes. Whenever we stop and look around, we may wonder "What's the hurry?" or "Where am I rushing to?" It's the hamster wheel. We hurry, hurry, hurry, and we don't really know why.

Vision changes that. The Bible says that where there is no vision, the people perish, but the person who keeps the law is happy. The New Living Translation says "When people do not accept divine guidance, they run wild. But whoever obeys the law is joyful." Vision sets a standard in our lives. It presents a goal, an outcome. The girl whose life is guided by the principles of God will have a Godly standard in her life. But the girl who wakes up and goes about her day with no vision in life will have no definite outcome. She doesn't know where she's going. How can she? There is no plan.

Do you have vision? Consider the principles guiding your life. Are they Godly? If you continue on the life path that you're on, what will be your outcome? Where there is no divine guidance, people perish. Are you following the divine guidance of God's Word?

In today's world, when we say we have a vision, we usually mean that we have a dream, a plan for the future. Visionaries are the movers and shakers of the world because they don't let the "hasn't been done" mean "it can't be done." Visionaries create and explore. They don't consider failure a shame, but a lesson. Vision gives them the resolve to try again. Vision is their anticipated outcome. Do you have an anticipated outcome? Is there a vision, a plan, for your life?

Many people in life are floaters. They float to work, they float home, they float to the TV screen, and then they float to bed. Nothing is motivating them to accomplish anything, because they have no vision for their life. Unless their goal is simply to watch TV, they are wasting much of the time given them.

Are you a floater or are you a visionary?

Scripture

Where there is no vision, the people perish: but he that keepeth the law, happy is he.

Proverbs 29:18

Action Step

1. Get a paper and pen. Are you following divine guidance or are you running on the hamster wheel? Write it down. Now choose which one you want to be doing. Write it down and circle it.
2. Are you a visionary or a floater? Write it down. Now choose what you want to be, write it down, and circle it.

Day 2

Lead Your Heart

We hear it all the time in movies. It's a slogan of our culture. "Follow your heart." Want to be famous? Follow your heart. Want to be a singer? Follow your heart. Want to go to the moon? Follow your heart. Want to find the love of your life? Follow your heart. Want to be a chimpanzee? Follow your heart. None of those things are wrong or bad. Though, the last one is impossible. But what do we actually mean when we say follow your heart? Follow your heart's *desires*, that's what we mean.

But think about it, are all your heart's desires good? My heart's desire may be to eat an entire bag of chocolate candy, but that's not necessarily good for me. Not all the desires of our hearts are positive things. Proverbs 23:19 tells us to guide our hearts. Guide means lead. How are we supposed to lead our hearts if we're following them? Sometimes, being a Christian woman means being counter-cultural. This is one of those cases.

In the day to day, are you following your heart or leading it? Do you weigh your decisions solely based on your own desires? Or do you consult God's Word, pray about it, or talk to wise, Godly people? If you were to follow your heart's every whim, where would you be headed? Where would you end up? Is it someplace good? But if you lead your heart, where will that get you? Probably somewhere much better.

Scripture

Hear thou, my son, and be wise, and guide thine heart in the way.
Proverbs 23:19

Action Step

1. Notice how you tend to make your decisions. Are you guiding your heart or following it? Now, choose to guide it in your decision-making from this day on.

Day 3

Body Image

Sometimes you might hate looking in the mirror. I know, I've been there too. It's hard to accept less than perfection in yourself. There's so much pressure in our culture to look a certain way. We've got this seemingly endless checklist of perfect body parts we must somehow attain and exhibit: flat belly, thigh gap, tan skin, white teeth, perfect hair, big boobs, perky butt, toned arms, oh yeah, and actually have a life while we're busy getting all those things.

It's unrealistic. Every body is different, and beauty is in the eye of the beholder anyway. What one person sees as beautiful perfection, another person may not even notice. That's actually the cool thing.

Every. Body. Is. Different.

Can you imagine how boring it'd be if every woman looked the same? Even if she was the most gorgeous thing in the world, it would get old fast. It's a reflection of God's creativity that no two women are exactly alike or exactly the same type of beautiful. You are a different beautiful from me, and I am a different beautiful from you! Isn't that just amazing?

You know, the crazy thing is, the more I learn to accept and love my body and my kind of beautiful, the more I see the beauty of the women around me. Try it! Look around and see all the different kinds of beautiful there actually is in the world. You might just be amazed. And then, look in the mirror. You'll find another kind of beautiful looking back at you.

Scripture

So shall the king greatly desire thy beauty: for he *is* thy Lord; and worship thou him.
Psalm 45:11

Action Step

1. Go look in the mirror. Notice each beautiful thing about yourself, perhaps your soft skin, high cheek bones, color of your eyes, the streaks in your hair, your lovely curves, the shape of your ears, the fullness of your lips. Drink in each detail of your beauty and go through your day with the knowledge that God's given you your own kind of beautiful.

Day 4

Be Still and Know

I'll tell you a secret. Sometimes, I slip out after dark and sit outside on my porch. All alone. The quiet and stillness speak to my soul. My mind wanders and I find myself talking to God. I think He meant it that way. When He said to be still and know that He is God, I think He put something inside us that needs time alone. When you're alone, undistracted, and still, you can hear better. You can think more clearly. You discover things. You can find yourself talking to Him. You can know . . . that He is God.

Our lives today are so BUSY. So distracted. So rushed. Sometimes it's hard to hear yourself think! Jobs, school, family, activities, church, friends, social media, it never ends. It can be hard to live intentionally when you're living at breakneck speed. It can be hard to respond to the Holy Spirit when you can't even feel His nudge. It can be hard to know He is God if you're never still.

So be still. Take time to be quiet. Turn off the distractions for a few minutes. Don't worry, they'll be there when you get back. Step away. Be still. Talk to God. Let Him talk to you. Know that He is God.

Scripture

He says, "Be still, and know that I am God; I will be exalted among the nations, I will be exalted in the earth."

Psalm 46:10 NIV

Action Step

1. Take time today to just be still. Step away from the noise and distraction and let your thoughts wander. Talk to God and allow Him to talk to you through His Spirit.

Day 5

Forgiveness

They say "forgive and forget." I kind of laugh and roll my eyes about that one. Yeah, forget? Like that's gonna happen.

Seriously, our brains aren't really wired to forget things. Things get embedded in our subconscious and it's not really possible to pluck them out of there. That's why I have another mantra when it comes to forgiveness. That mantra is "I release you from what you owe me."

Suppose someone hurts my family, and I am having a hard time forgiving them. "Forgive and forget" doesn't help. There's no chance I'm going to forget about it. But I've learned that, although I can't forget, and perhaps they aren't even sorry, I can release them from the debt they owe me. Do they owe an apology? Of course, they hurt my family. Should they repent and ask forgiveness? Of course, they wronged someone by what they did. Should they try to make reparations? Of course, they committed an error. But I can release them from those things. I can forgive the debt that I feel they owe me. Will I forget what they did? Nope. But I don't have to be chained to that person by their wrong that they committed. I can free myself. I'm not doing it for them, I'm forgiving them for *me*. So that I don't have to be filled with bitterness and anger. I can have peace and joy and move on in my life without allowing them to hold me back.

Is there someone in your life you need to forgive? Take this mantra as your own "I release you from what you owe me." Unforgiveness hurts you more than the other person. Free yourself. Liberate yourself from the sins of the other person.

Scripture

And forgive us our debts, as we forgive our debtors.

Matthew 6:12

Action Step

1. If there is someone in your life whom you haven't forgiven, release them from their debts. Live in the freedom of being tied to no one and having a joyous, peaceful heart.

Day 6

Life-Giving Tongue

Proverbs 18:21: "The tongue has the power of life and death, and those that love it will eat its fruit." Words have power. They can give someone life, or bring them death. The old adage "Sticks and stones may break my bones, but words can never hurt me" is nothing but a big lie. Words do hurt. A lot. They can crush a person's spirit. "The words of the reckless pierce like swords, but the tongue of the wise brings healing," says Proverbs 12:18. Reckless words are painful. Statements with no previous thought just flung into the wind. No concern for the listener. Dripping candidness. Over indulgences. Broken trusts.

What does it mean to have a life-giving tongue? It's the intentional practice of bringing healing, encouragement, wisdom, affirmation, and comfort through our words. *Healing*; it means remedy, sound, wholesome, yielding, curative, deliverance (Strong's Exhaustive Concordance).

A tongue that gives life encourages others, it builds people up and lets them know someone believes in them and is in their corner. It's affirming, communicating that "you're okay," "good job," "you've got this," and "I believe in you." It builds up their spirit. A life-giving tongue is wise, or at the very least, committed to getting wiser. It provides comfort for those in pain, whether it's physical or emotional pain. Comfort will bring solace to a hurting person like a hand reaching down to help them back up when they've fallen. Life-giving words can bring healing to places that have been wounded. "I'm here for the long haul," "You're making a difference," "Thank you for...," "You're beautiful," "I love you anyway," "We'll get through this," "You matter to me," " I'm so glad God gave you to me." These are words that can bring hope or healing. God is the ultimate healer. But we can be his tools here on earth to help mend each other's broken spirits

Scripture

The tongue has the power of life and death, and those that love it will eat its fruit.

Proverbs 18:21

Action Step

1. Have a life-giving tongue. Use your words to affirm or help heal someone's spirit today.

Day 7

Fear

Fear is an alert for danger. We fear snakes because we don't want to get hurt. We fear bees and scorpions because we don't want to get stung. But, many times we are afraid of things that are not actually dangerous, they just don't feel very good. Often, though, we can learn from those things, and do better the next time.

It's not about not being afraid. I'm not sure that fear ever really goes away, it only lessens. So, it's not about eradicating fear, but overcoming it. That's called courage, or bravery, when you're afraid and you still forge ahead. It's courageous to stick your neck out and do something that people could judge you for. It's courageous to do the right thing when others aren't. It's courageous to stand up for someone else. It's courageous to stand up for yourself. It's courageous to forgive someone who isn't sorry. It's courageous to get hurt and still love people. It's courageous to live out your own beliefs. It's courageous to step out of other people's expectations of you. It's courageous to live free from Doubt and low self-esteem. It's courageous to be afraid and do it anyway. "Courage is not the absence of fear, but rather the assessment that something else is more important than fear." - Franklin D. Roosevelt. (Excerpt taken from *Self-Esteem* by Meagan Trayler.)

What is something you've been too afraid to do, but know it's right, would be good for you, or that you've been wanting to do? Is staying in your comfort zone more important than that thing?

Scripture

So do not fear, for I am with you; do not be dismayed, for I am your God. I will strengthen you and help you; I will uphold you with my righteous right hand.

Isaiah 41:10 NIV

Action Step

1. List things that you're afraid of. Are these things truly dangerous or do they just not feel good?
2. Be brave today and face one of those fears that don't feel very good. Notice how you feel afterward: confident, proud, brave, powerful, triumphant, or tall?

Day 8

Doubt

Doubt tells us we aren't good enough, that we'll never measure up. Doubt is a self-talk voice that talks really, really loud, screams even. He knows our weaknesses and our vulnerabilities. He targets just the right spots. He can make us believe whatever he wants if we let him. But he's a fraud and a lie. Doubt is a tool of Satan, and Satan is the Father of lies, according to John 8:44. Satan uses doubt, low self-esteem, lies, fear, whatever he can, to hold us back from reaching our potential and living a life of freedom and Godliness.

Doubt is born of fear. We fear we won't measure up, so we doubt we will. We fear failure, so we don't even try. We fear embarrassment, so we hang back. We fear danger, so we play it safe. So, this is my challenge to you, and to me - be afraid and do it anyway. That thing on your heart that you want to do, or think you ought to do, or that God is calling you to do, be afraid and just do it. If it's something you care about, something that's important to you, failure to try is still failure. What's the worst thing that could happen? Think about it. Does the worst thing that could happen outweigh the potential rewards of attempting it? Does the regret outweigh the risk? (Excerpt taken from *Self-Esteem* by Meagan Trayler.)

Scripture

But when you ask, you must believe and not doubt, because the one who doubts is like a wave of the sea, blown and tossed by the wind

James 1:6 NIV

Action Step

1. Defeat doubt and do that thing on your heart that you've been putting off. Take action today.

Day 9

Be A Life-Giver

According to Strong's Concordance, Eve means "life." At the very essence of womanhood is the gift of being a life-giver. We are nurturers. Our very bodies are built to give life.

But you do not have to have children to use your power as a life-giver. You can use your words, touch, actions, attitude, and character to be a life-giver right now! Your words can life-giving, affirming, loving, or full of negativity, doubt, and complaints. Your touch can be harsh or gentle. Your actions can be unkind and hurtful, or loving and full of good. Your attitude can be positive and cheerful, or negative and ugly. Your character can be strong, Godly, and honest, or weak, worldly, and deceitful.

You have the incredible capacity to give life to those around you. You can mentor younger girls, reach out to friends, even minister to a stranger. There are so many ways to give life to those around you. Simply using your words to encourage someone, or your actions to help someone, can bring a boost of joy and life to their day.

Have you ever been in the room with someone who constantly talks negatively? All they do is issue complaint after complaint or criticism after criticism. After awhile you might have to leave the room because you just can't take the toxic environment anymore! That person is being a Death-Bringer instead of a Life-Giver. Be the opposite and fill the space around you with joy and peace.

Scripture

And Adam called his wife's name Eve; because she was the mother of all living

Genesis 3:20

Action Step

1. Consider your role as a Life-Giver. Make a list of ways you can give life to those around you. Look for opportunities to be a Life-Giver today.

Day 10

Pursuing Excellence

By always learning and growing in knowledge of something or skill in something, you will use and not waste the abilities God's given you. God has not given us talents and interests just to make life more fun. I believe the passions He's put inside you are paths to follow to loving people, loving yourself, and loving God. Those things are called ministry, fulfillment, and worship.

For example, I love words and music, so I try to use those things to bless others and praise God. Whatever interests or talents you have, there's always a way to use them as blessings, instead of keeping them to yourself.

When you continue to learn and grow, you'll also be more interesting as a person. Someone with diverse experiences and pursuits would have much more to offer in a conversation and life in general. The more you know about something, the more knowledge you can share with people. The more experiences you've had, the more information you can share with people. No one has the intention to be boring, but if we do nothing with our lives other than waste our time, that's eventually what we become! You're never too young to get better at something. You're never too young to learn more about something. With the amazing brains God's given us, we have the capacity to learn nearly anything we decide to. (Excerpt taken from *Self-Esteem* by Meagan Trayler.)

Are you pursuing excellence in your life? What are your skills or passions that you're currently developing? How can you use them for ministry, fulfillment, or worship?

Scripture

For this very reason, make every effort to add to your faith goodness; and to goodness, knowledge; and to knowledge, self-control; and to self-control, perseverance; and to perseverance, godliness; and to godliness, mutual affection; and to mutual affection, love. For if you possess these qualities in increasing measure, they will keep you from being ineffective and unproductive in your knowledge of our Lord Jesus Christ.

2 Peter 1:5-8

Action Step

1. List some things you're good at. Now, beside each one write down ways you can use those gifts to minister to others, fulfill yourself, and worship God.

Day 11

Embrace Your Uniqueness

There is no one else exactly like you. You are unique. I am unique. Yet, sometimes we're afraid to be ourselves. Maybe that's because we're afraid of what people will think of us, we're afraid they won't like us, or we don't think we're good enough just as "us." Maybe we want that certain person to like us, or be our friend, so we change ourselves trying to be someone we're not. But we're not authentic when we're trying to be someone else. We can admire good character or qualities in another person and try to emulate them. That's great! But to try to become exactly like someone else is impossible. Not only that, God made you with unique abilities and interests on purpose. Disregarding who you are in an effort to be someone else in an insult to your Creator.

So, who are you? What makes you, you? What makes you tick? What causes you to jump for joy? What pushes your buttons? What needs do you have? What are the best ways to take care of yourself? In what environments do you operate the best? What lights your fire? What do you want to leave behind?

Learning to embrace who you are is important. You'll never be anybody else. Whatever intricacies that are unique to you are there on purpose. Discover them, and then embrace them. Once you do, find ways to challenge yourself. Find things you want to be good at. Look for someone to invest in. Search for ways to make the world more beautiful. These pursuits will give your life personal passion and purpose. Only within the realms of knowing and embracing who you are, and loving God, and blessing others, will you find true joy and fulfillment. (Excerpt taken from *Self-Esteem* by Meagan Trayler.)

Scripture

But now, O LORD, thou *art* our father; we *are* the clay, and thou our potter; and we all *are* the work of thy hand.

Isaiah 64:8

Action Step

1. Reflect on yourself for a moment and answer the questions in the last paragraph. If you don't have a specific answer to each that's okay. Just write something that you know is personal to you.

Day 12

Nurturing Relationships

Some friends come and then they go. Others stay with you for a lifetime. Strange, the way life works out sometimes.

When I was in college I had a small group of . . . let's say acquaintances. We were all in the music program and hung out frequently. But I never really was *in*, you know? Now, we've gone our separate ways and I haven't heard a thing from any of them in years. But you know who is still very much in my life? My high school literature teacher, my sisters, my Mom, girls at church who are in the same stage of life as me, friends who I only see a few times a year but who always pick up right where we left off. Those are the ones I call when I'm crying, when I need a night off and someone to laugh with, when I'm excited and want to share some good news, the ones who'll pick me up on the side of the road when my car breaks down, and when I need some wise advice. Those are the relationships that last.

Who in your life has been there for you in the hard times? Who is always there when you need someone to talk to? Who would pick you up late at night on the side of the road? Who accepts you for you and loves you to the moon and back? Who has been there for you when no one else was around? Those are the relationships that'll last. Take care of them. Nurture them. They are what makes life meaningful.

Scripture

There are "friends" who destroy each other, but a real friend sticks closer than a brother.

Proverbs 18:24 NLT

Action Step

1. Send a text, meet up, or write a card to a friend today. Let them know you appreciate your friendship.

Day 13

Your Purpose for Dating

What do you want out of a relationship? Are you genuinely looking for a potential spouse? Or are you bored, really wanting a recreational relationship? Are you seeking affirmation, value, or confidence, and you think a guy can give you those things? Do you think it's what you're "supposed" to do? You're 16, 18, 25, whatever age, and people are expecting you to have a boyfriend or get married soon. So, you just play along, even though you're not sure if it's what you actually want or are ready for? Do you not really know what else to do with your life, and you think that one option is as good as another . . .

In other words, are you desperate, or are you truly seeking a potential husband? We are supposed to do everything to the glory of God (1 Cor 10:31). Looking for a guy just to mess around with, play with his emotions, and waste time, isn't for God's glory.

Marriage, on the other hand, is created and blessed by God. It's holy and sacred (Heb 13:4).

Carefully considering a spouse is something right and good, and not just that, it's WISE! Playing around with the opposite sex will only end with broken emotions, strained relationships, and the loss of precious time.

What is your purpose for dating? Are you desperate? Are you really looking for a husband? Are you ready to use wisdom and discernment in your long-term choices? Are you ready to hold someone else's heart in your hands?

. . . what is your purpose for dating?

Scripture

The woman who is unmarried, and the virgin, is concerned about the things of the Lord, that she may be holy both in body and spirit;

1 Corinthians 7:34B

Action Step

1. Write down several reasons for your dating relationship or your desire to have one. Are they good, mature, or holy reasons, or are they desperate, immature, impure reasons?

Day 14

You're Not Alone

Whatever you're going through right now, you are not alone. Sometimes, it seems like we are the only one who's gone through what we're going through. But I want you to know that that's not true.

The Bible says there is nothing new under the sun (Ecc 1:9). What you are feeling has been felt before. What you're struggling with has been struggled through by someone else. Your desires have been someone else's desires. And your heartbreak has been felt in another's chest. You are not alone.

God gave us community in family and the church to have a built-in support group. Reach out. Share with someone you trust what you're going through. They often can give you counsel, or loving empathy. Others who have gone before us know the way. They've been through the valleys and still reached the mountaintops. Many are willing to reach back and hold your hand to pull you up beside them.

Being a teen, preteen, or young person in general, can be hard. Growing up is hard. Relationships are hard. Moving on is hard. Being a young parent is hard. Losing someone you care about is hard. Making decisions is hard. Sometimes, even loving yourself is hard. But you are not alone. Others have gone before you, and know the way.

Scripture

If one person falls, the other can reach out and help. But someone who falls alone is in real trouble.
Ecclesiastes 4:10 NLT

Action Step

1. List names of people you trust who you can reach out to when life is hard.

Day 15

You Are Enough

Sometimes young people have no one speaking truth into their lives; no one who will talk about their innate worth. And so, when they look to a cruel cyber world for their value, they are left with a void ripe for depression, and if left unaddressed, self-harm or suicide. Something has to be done about this. I am here to tell you that this is not the path to self-worth, and I can tell you what is . . .

A relationship with your Creator. Worth and value come from God. Simply because you are a human being you are worthy. God said "Let us make mankind in our image . . . " [4] We are created as representations, or images, of God. You are valuable, you are enough, simply because you are human, made in God's image. There's nothing you have to prove. There's nothing you have to change. There's nothing you have to do to be worthy. You already are.

(Excerpt from *Self-Esteem* by Meagan Trayler.)

Scripture

Then God said, "Let us make mankind in our image, in our likeness..."

Genesis 1:26A

Action Step

1. Make a list of ways that you are unique. Make another list that describe who you are in God (daughter, chosen, loved, forgiven, created wonderfully, etc.)

Day 16

Be Of Use

I have a friend who feels called to serve others and love people in whatever way she can. For example, she's gone on a mission trip to Africa and helped rescue people in the wake of a destructive hurricane. I respect this girl very much because she has not only taken her life and calling seriously, she has used her time and talents for God and others and hasn't wasted them. Instead of thinking, "Oh, someone else will probably do it" she got out there and started helping, working and serving others. This is exactly what we need to be doing, using whatever we have, whether that's talent, money, energy, or simply our time and willingness, to give back. I asked her to write about her experiences in loving God and serving others. This is an excerpt of what she wrote:

> In a world where there is so much ugly, I feel the responsibility to spread beauty. Not only in my circle, my space, my comfort zone but everywhere. I believe two of the most beautiful things you can do in this world are to love and serve others. I often struggle with how to do this. So many times, I find myself only wanting to serve in "big ways" when serving small can make just as big of an impact.
>
> In 2014 I was given the opportunity to go on my first ever mission trip to Kenya, Africa. I

was ecstatic and also very nervous not knowing what to expect. My parents, especially my dad, did not want me to go because they felt I was putting myself at risk for danger. I didn't care. I was going to go and no one was going to stop me. While in Africa, a brother gave an amazing lesson that brought me to tears. It was on Isaiah 6:8 which says, "Then I heard the voice of the Lord saying, 'Whom shall I send? And who will go for us?' And I said, 'Here am I. Send me!'" God is looking for faithful men and women to accomplish His will and purpose on Earth. He uses willing and obedient servants, people who make themselves available to God's call upon their lives to build His kingdom.

Being of use to others was something I had always had an interest in but I didn't really know how to go about it. I was only focused on the bigger ways to help and be of service. Because of this I didn't give it a whole lot of thought . . . [But] I felt it was something I needed to be doing as a Christian. And not just that, I wanted to.

She is right. May we all be that person that says, "Here I am, send me!" (Excerpt taken *Self-Esteem* by Meagan Trayler.)

Scripture

Then I heard the voice of the Lord saying, "Whom shall I send? And who will go for us?" And I said, "Here am I. Send me!"

Isaiah 6:8 NIV

Action Step

1. Think about ways you can be of use today. Choose one and make it happen.

Day 17

Choosing Joy

Someone once told me that if they pointed out a clump of flowers, I would reply that they were wilted. I am very prone to negativity, stress, worry, and tension. So, two of the major mental battles I've fought have been releasing negativity and choosing joy. I consciously let negativity go, and choose to be joyful. Now, that does not mean I am always happy. It does not mean I go around with a plastic smile, pretending things are okay when they're not. What it does mean is that I try to notice and appreciate the positive, like a vibrant sunset, my baby girls' laughter, a cup of coffee and some homemade muffins, a good book, a rainy day at home . . . I do things and take time for things that refresh my spirit. It takes some practice to get into the habit of looking for the positive, instead of dwelling on the negative, but it gets easier and more natural as you continue to do it.

Do you choose joy? Do you remind yourself that today is the day the Lord has made, and you will rejoice and be glad in it? (Psalm 118:24). Do you allow negativity and dark thoughts to consume you day after day? It's easy, so easy. Joy takes intention. It takes practice. It takes a decision. But it all starts small. Today. You can make the decision to have joy today. Look for the positive. Be grateful. Smile. Say thank you. Do something you enjoy. Thank God for what you have. (Excerpt from *Self-Esteem* by Meagan Trayler.)

Scripture

This *is* the day *which* the LORD hath made; we will rejoice and be glad in it.

Psalm 118:24

Action Step

1. Decide that today you will choose joy. Begin by looking for the positive.

Day 18

Deepest Cuts

Life can hurt. Pain and regrets break our hearts. Depression can enfold us like a dark cloud. We don't know what to do with our emotions sometimes. We may intentionally hurt ourselves. We may add pain to pain, because we don't know how to deal with the first one. Life can be rough, like a raging sea or roaring fire. We may feel we're being drowned or burned alive.

It's hard to know what to do sometimes. It's hard to know how to handle certain situations. Decisions to make, or decisions we've made, may cause us constant grief. Experiences may cut us, both emotionally and physically, seen and unseen. And though deep cuts heal, they still leave scars. Life can be hard, because we're not meant to stay here. Hebrews 13:14 says "For this world is not our permanent home; we are looking forward to a home yet to come." (NLT) This world is a temporary, and sometimes rough, place to be.

But there is comfort for those times. God says "When you go through deep waters, I will be with you. When you go through rivers of difficulty, you will not drown. When you walk through the fire of oppression, you will not be burned up; the flames will not consume you." (NLT) For those deepest cuts, God will be there.

Scripture

When you pass through the waters, I will be with you; and when you pass through the rivers, they will not sweep over you. When you walk through the fire, you will not be burned; the flames will not set you ablaze.
Isaiah 43:2 NIV

Action Step

1. Think about a rough time in your life. Can you see God's hand in it? Were there people who were His face to you, His arms to hold you, His voice comforting you?

Day 19

The Comparison Trap

You walk into a room, and scope out every girl there to see how you measure up. I've done the same. You give every girl, including yourself, a rating based on good looks, body, and fashion. Probably every girl in the world has done this. But, I've gotta tell ya, it's a trap.

The Comparison Trap. Old as the ages. Genesis 29:1: "And Leah's eyes were weak, but Rachel was beautiful of form and face." (NASB) Women have an innate desire to be beautiful, but that desire can easily turn into a Beauty Queen Competition real fast. If you play the game and lose, you're depressed, resentful, bitter, envious, and ungrateful for the incredible gift of body and beauty God has given you. If you win, you're proud, vain, haughty, and unloving to the women God's placed in your life. Either way, win or lose, you lose. In neither instance do you become more loving, more grateful, more joyful, more Godly, more gracious, more humble, or more affirming. You lose respect and appreciation for yourself, and those around you. It's a trap. Don't play the game.

Instead, try complimenting people, both yourself and others. It brings me so much happiness to be in a store, standing in the checkout line, and be given the opportunity to compliment the cashier. It totally makes someone's day to be complimented! And it's so easy. You could totally change a person's world at that moment and *you* hold all the power.

Same goes for you. God specifically gave you certain characteristics that He's not given to others. Embrace what gifts He's given you and use them with thankfulness. Compliment yourself. Appreciate the compliment. Relish the beauty God deigned to bestow on you. It can be hard to see past everything you want changed. But look at the gifts you have. Value them. And don't fall into the trap. Refuse to play the game.

Scripture

We do not dare to classify or compare ourselves with some who commend themselves. When they measure themselves by themselves and compare themselves with themselves, they are not wise.

2 Corinthians 10:12

Action Step

1. Give someone a genuine compliment today. And if you fall into the comparison trap, mentally give each person a compliment, including yourself.

Day 20

Do Him Good

Lots of little girls dream about wearing a white dress and walking down the aisle. They may even play act it with their sisters and friends, sometimes snagging a little boy to play the groom's part. It's all pretend. But in their little girl minds, it will happen someday, they just need to find the missing piece. The piece that's always a little hazy. The guy.

There's something about wearing all white. And our culture has made it so very special. It's something we put on for one person, in one moment of our lives. But did you know that you can do something about that hazy, missing piece before you ever meet him? Proverbs 31:12 says "She brings him good, not harm, all the days of her life." (NIV) Did you catch that? It says ALL the days of her life. *All*, as in, right now. At this very moment. Well, how in the world are you supposed to do him good when you don't even know who in the world he is? Good question.

A way you can do him good is to pray for him. Pray for his maturity, Godliness, wisdom, work ethic, soft-heartedness, Bible knowledge, fatherliness, compassion, tenderness, integrity, and character. Pray for him to be a man of God, with a strong character, an open, humble heart, and selflessness.

Also, you can do him good right now by working on yourself. Strive to become the strong, Christian woman that you ought to be. Study your Bible, practice loving others, being humble, and ministering to people around you. Read books, be healthy, have experiences, grow as a person, set goals and accomplish them. Don't waste your time sitting around waiting on Prince Charming. Live your life and become a vibrant, loving, Godly woman. Your groom may someday join your life as a complementary piece, but he'll not join it to complete you. Live your life as a whole person. And perhaps, someday, another whole person will join you on life's journey.

Scripture

She will do him good and not evil all the days of her life.

Proverbs 31:12

Action Step

1. What are some ways you can do your (potential) future husband good today?

Day 21

Self-Talk

Self-talk, specifically negative self-talk, is the silent conversation you're always having with yourself. You might look in the mirror while you put on your makeup and you tell yourself, for the thousandth time, how big your nose is. You may struggle to grasp a specific concept and then berate yourself for how stupid you are. You try to do a task as best you can, but when you make a mistake a little voice whispers "you'll never be good enough."

Silence the voice! This is your battle to win. Create a habit of turning off the negative self-talk and replacing it with positive self-talk. What you replace it with, specifically, is up to you. Positive self-talk, affirmation, prayer, reciting scripture, redirecting to more neutral thoughts, reading, starting a conversation, finding things you're thankful for, are all ways to replace negative self-talk. I'm sure you can come up with plenty more. Find a replacement technique that works for you, or several if you want to, and replace the negative self-talk every time you catch yourself doing it. Don't let you be mean to yourself.

If you're in the habit of self-criticizing or negative self-talk, practice recognizing those thoughts, and then replacing them with a positive one. If you catch yourself criticizing a personal feature you don't particularly like, for instance, dismiss that thought and replace it with a thought of a feature you do like. It's not prideful. It's healthy. Getting out of the downward spiral of negative self-talk is difficult, but so necessary to living a balanced, healthy life. It's in the mind that battles are won and lost. Taking ownership for our thought lives is the first step to victory. (Excerpt from *Self-Esteem* by Meagan Trayler.)

Scripture

Finally, brothers, whatever is true, whatever is honorable, whatever is just, whatever is pure, whatever is lovely, whatever is commendable, if there is any excellence, if there is anything worthy of praise, think about these things.

Philippians 4:8 ESV

Action Step

1. Choose at least one replacement technique to use when you find yourself using negative self-talk.

Day 22

Step Outside the Drama

There's always drama somewhere, in family, church, social media, or friendships. Usually, it does nothing but cause hurt feelings, pride, gossip, and strained relationships. Unless you're smack dab in the middle of it, get out. If you are in the middle of it, own your part, make amends, and try to make peace. You'll be more confident knowing that you yourself did the right thing and tried your best to resolve conflict. You can then be at peace with yourself. If you aren't in the middle of it, try not to get involved, unless absolutely necessary. Just stay away.

Sometimes, to stay out of the mess, you might need to create some space. Depending on the situation, this might mean avoiding, but of course being respectful to, certain family members, hanging out with different friends, getting off or limiting social media, or something along those lines. Remember, none of these things have to be forever, could be only for a little while. You'll be glad you saved yourself some headache and heartache in the meantime. Sometimes, the most loving thing you can do for others and yourself, is to love them from afar. The Apostle Paul said in 1 Corinthians 3 that divisions and quarrels mean we are worldly and acting like sinful people. Try to stay out of the drama. You will grow in confidence, knowing that you're taking control of your own direction in life, steering clear of some of its pitfalls. (Excerpt from *Self-Esteem* by Meagan Trayler.)

Scripture

[F]or you are still controlled by your sinful nature. You are jealous of one another and quarrel with each other. Doesn't that prove you are controlled by your sinful nature? Aren't you living like people of the world?

1 Corinthians 3:3 NLT

Action Step

1. Is there drama in your life you need to get out of? If you can, figure out how to gracefully bow out of it. If you're right in the middle, own your part, apologize, and be a peacemaker.

Day 23

Made on Purpose

You aren't an accident. You were planned and made on purpose. God was not surprised by you. He timed your birth with precision. Jeremiah 1:5 says "Before I formed you in the womb I knew you" (NIV). Do you know what that means? *Before* you were even a physical object on this planet, He knew who you were. Isn't that incredible?

Psalm 139:13-14 reads "For you created my inmost being; you knit me together in my mother's womb. I praise you because I am fearfully and wonderfully made; your works are wonderful, I know that full well." Whether your parents planned you or not, whether anyone on this earth was surprised by you or not, you were planned by an unsurprised God.

You were made on purpose. I heard someone once say that "God doesn't say oops." It's true. God is God. He doesn't make accidents. You're here on purpose. Rest on that fact today.

Scripture

"Before I formed you in the womb I knew you, before you were born I set you apart; I appointed you as a prophet to the nations."
Jeremiah 1:5 NIV

Action Step

1. Get a notecard, sticky note, or small piece of paper. Write on it "Made on Purpose" and put it somewhere you'll see it through out your day: on your mirror, beside your bed, in a book, on the fridge, or in your car.

Day 24

Acknowledge Him

Do you ever use a GPS? If you're used to using one when you drive, you might feel lost without one, even if you're not lost. I depend on mine all the time. It's become my new best friend when I'm on the road. I don't know how I'd live without it.

There is something about being lost that frightens people. I guess it's the unknown; the uncertainty. The fear that they will never get back home, back within their comfort zone. I get it. Being lost on the road terrifies me. Forging ahead without a plan, or a guide, is unthinkable. My GPS is my guide on the road. But what's the guide for my life?

Do you have a GPS in your life? Not in your car, but your life. While we love to use the Global Positioning System while driving, do we use God's Perfect System in our lives? What exactly IS God's Perfect System you ask? I'll tell you. It's this: "Always let him lead you, and he will clear the road for you to follow" (CEV). There you have it, your life's GPS, not to be confused with your vehicle's GPS.

Do you let God lead you? Do you ask him to show you which way to go, which path to take? Do you consult him and his roadmap when you're going somewhere? If you acknowledge him in everything you do, he *will* guide you. That's the GPS, God's Perfect System.

Scripture

In all thy ways acknowledge him, and he shall direct thy paths.

Proverbs 3:6

Action Step

1. Do you use God's Perfect System in your life? If not, start using it today and acknowledge him in everything you do.

Day 25

It's a Heart Issue

It's a heart issue. I've heard it numerous times. It means that Christianity is a matter of the heart. It's a matter of being truly converted, *really convicted*, in your heart to the Bible, to the truth. To do something wholeheartedly is to do something with full faith and without reserve. To do something with your heart is to associate meaning and value to it. Without the heart, without full conviction and measure of faith, Christianity becomes only a "religion" to be studied impartially, or a set of restrictive rules. When faith isn't a heart issue, Christianity becomes a tradition handed down to us, like culture or heirlooms.

Is Christianity a tradition in your life? Is it something interesting to be studied impartially, as a scholar would an ancient document? Or is Christianity a purpose-driven, desperate searching, achingly got-to-find quest for the truth in life? If faith is a lifestyle for you, which is very easy to fall in to, find your reasons for your faith again. Why is it YOUR faith? Because you've studied the evidence? Because you've read about the historicity of Jesus? Because you've looked at evidence of Intelligent Design? Why is your faith . . . yours?

It's a heart issue. Without conviction, it's not real. It all comes down to the heart.

Scripture

I will give you a new heart and put a new spirit in you; I will remove from you your heart of stone and give you a heart of flesh.

Ezekiel 36:26 NIV

Action Step

1. What is Christianity to you? Why is your faith YOUR faith? Write down your answers.

Day 26

Be a Leader

They were shopping for gowns: the bride, the mother of the bride, and all the bridesmaids. While perusing a bridal shop, the young bridesmaids began critiquing themselves in the full-length mirrors that spanned the walls. As the girls were pointing out their flaws and complaining about their appearance, one of them suddenly spoke.

"If you can't say *one* nice thing about yourselves, you're not allowed to look in the mirror anymore!"

She was tall, confident, and spoke with the authority of one who is comfortable in her own skin. She broke the status quo and became a leader of her generation in that moment. The girls refrained from further negative statements, due to the strength and confidence of one girl.

We should all be like this young lady. We should all strive to have the strength, courage, and wisdom to speak out into our generation and be a voice of truth. Like her, we should each be the anomaly that embraces Godliness, true beauty, quiet confidence, and bravery.

Be a leader. Use your voice to speak truth into the world. Be a change-maker. Be a mover and shaker. Be brave. Be clothed with strength and dignity. Be an anomaly.

Scripture

Don't let anyone look down on you because you are young, but set an example for the believers in speech, in conduct, in love, in faith and in purity.

1 Timothy 4:12 NIV

Action Step

1. Look for ways to be a leader today. Speak truth into your generation.

Day 27

Feelings-Tricky Little Things

While I used to believe that feelings have a life of their own and we have absolutely no control over them, I now know differently. I once thought that emotions were simply based on circumstances. They come and go at will, and we simply have to feel them, stuff them, or numb them, and then let them go. To some extent, this is true. Some emotions are so big, so real, so *visceral*, that in order for them to pass on we must fully experience and deal with them, before they can pass. (And, by the way, stuffing or numbing emotions is not okay. They usually come back to haunt us in the forms of anxiety, bad habits, addictions, outbursts of anger, or illness.)

But, while I used to believe that we are at the mercy of our emotions, I've since learned that emotions are based on *what we think*. That's right, you get to *choose* your emotions, based on the *thoughts* you choose to think. I learned this from the Life Coach School. While most people think that their feelings or emotions are based on their circumstances (I got a D on that test, I lost my job, my pet died, my friend is mad at me, etc.) the truth is that we have a lot more control over our feelings than we think. Because by choosing different thoughts, we change how we feel. For example, if my pet died, I could think "I can't believe she's gone. I miss her so much. I'll never love another animal like I loved her. I can't believe this has happened." These kinds of thoughts will create feelings of heartbreak, loneliness, despair, denial, and hopelessness. But if, instead, I think thoughts like "She had a good, long life. She was old and tired. I'm glad she's not in pain anymore. I'm glad we had so many years together. Someday I'll be ready for another pet, but for now, I'm going to remember her." These thoughts create much different emotions that the previous ones. I can completely change how I feel about a situation simply by choosing different thoughts. And you can, too.

Scripture

Finally, brothers and sisters, whatever is true, whatever is noble, whatever is right, whatever is pure, whatever is lovely, whatever is admirable — if anything is excellent or praiseworthy — think about such things.

Phil 4:8 NIV

Action Step

1. What are you feeling today? What thoughts are you choosing in order to feel this way? Do these thoughts and feelings serve you? What thoughts could you choose that would create feelings that you would like better? Write down your answers to these questions.

Day 28

Respect is a Reflection of You

Not much shows the heart of a person more than the way they treat others. Truly, how a person treats someone else says more about them than the other person. So, treat others well. I know we're all human, we're all selfish, sinful, and proud. We're not always going to treat others in a way that communicates to them that they are valuable and worthy. But we must try. Talk to people with courtesy, respect, and self-control.

Respect is really just communicating to another person that you acknowledge their value, either as a human being, or as someone in their unique position. Respect doesn't mean kiss up, be a door mat, or give up rights. It's how you would treat a stranger. You'd say please and thank you, hold open the door, control your words and tone, be courteous.

Often, we treat our own families worse than people we're never going to see again. It shouldn't be that way. Do you respect your parents? Do you use words and your tone in ways that tell them you are listening to what they have to say, whether or not you agree with them? Are you flippant and proud towards them, insinuating that you know better and couldn't care less what they think? Do you treat your siblings well? Or do you make them feel small, stupid, or unloved? Home and family are where you learn and lay the groundwork for all the relationships you'll ever have in life. How you talk to and treat others is a reflection of yourself. What are you reflecting?

Scripture

Show proper respect to everyone, love the family of believers, fear God, honor the emperor.
1 Peter 2:17 NIV

Action Step

1. Resolve to treat everyone with courtesy today, no matter what.

Day 29

What Are You Wearing?

I know what you're thinking, and no, that's not what I'm talking about. I don't mean the clothes on your body; I'm talking about the other things you're wearing. We wear lots of things that don't actually hang in our closets. But, like the clothes in our closets, we *choose* what we wear.

The Bible says "All of you, clothe yourselves with humility toward one another, because, "God opposes the proud but shows favor to the humble" (1 Peter 5:5 NIV). When you woke up today, did you put on pride or humility? You probably didn't even think about it, but whether you consciously chose one or not, you're wearing one on your attitude right now. Which one is it?

There are other items the Bible tells us to wear. Colossians 3:12 says "Therefore, as God's chosen people, holy and dearly loved, clothe yourselves with compassion, kindness, humility, gentleness and patience." Did you put on any of those this morning? If you didn't, put them on now. Decide that when someone needs empathy or understanding, you will be compassionate. When someone is hurting be gentle and kind. When someone is slow or frustrating, be patient.

Lastly, wear love. "Above all, clothe yourselves with love, which binds us all together in perfect harmony" (Colossians 3:14 NLT). This is the most important item to wear. It's not always natural to wear it. It doesn't always feel comfortable or seem to fit right. But it's the most beautiful item in your closet, and it ought to be the first thing we put on every day.

Scripture

She is clothed with strength and dignity, and she laughs without fear of the future.

Proverbs 31:25 NLT

Action Step

1. Think about which of these items you usually wear throughout your day. Now make a list of the items that you don't wear much, or at all, and place it in or beside your closet so you'll see every time you get dressed. Use it as a reminder to dress your spirit as well as your body.

Day 30

Be Your Whole You

I read something once which I've never forgotten. It said "Be Somebody, before you're Somebody's."

Let's say that someday one of my baby girls gets married. She might marry an amazing, wonderful guy. But no matter how wonderful he is, he cannot make her a Somebody if she isn't already. He can't give her enough affirmation, affection, or attention that'll make her "enough." If she doesn't realize that she is already innately valuable, she'll look to him, as I did to my boyfriend, to determine her worth. But he will never be able fulfill the need inside her to know that she is worthy. Her husband will never be able to bear the burden of her lack of self-esteem. It's too much for any individual to bear the load of someone else's self-worth. Do you know what the great thing is? She's already enough. She's just got to own it. Own the worth that God's already given her.

(. . .) We are the wildly loved children of a God. We are worthy and valuable and enough because of God. Made in His image and adopted as His daughters, we are enough. *You* are enough. When my baby girls have accepted these truths and really believe them, then they can be whole, complete people. Then they will be Somebody, and so will you. (Excerpt from *Self-Esteem* by Meagan Trayler)

You do not need a guy to make you good enough. You don't need to be prettier to be good enough. There is nothing you need to make you good enough. You, alone, are GOOD ENOUGH. Don't ever forget that. Don't ever doubt that. God created you, so you are *very good* (Gen 1:31). Remember, be Somebody before you're Somebody's!

Scripture

Then God said, "Let us make mankind in our image, in our likeness . . .

Genesis 1:26A NIV

Action Step

1. Write down in BIG, BOLD letters "I Am Enough."
2. Write down "Be Somebody Before You're Somebody's" in colorful ink or pencils.

Author's Note

Reader, thank you for reading this devotional. I hope it has blessed and encouraged you over the last month. I hope you will continue growing in your spiritual journey through Bible reading and study. And don't forget, coffee and Bible go together!

Meagan Trayler

Did you enjoy this book? Please leave me a positive review!

Search for this book on Amazon.com and let me know what you think!

Want More?

Other books by Meagan Trayler:

Self-Esteem: The Teen Girl's Journey to Self-Worth, Body Image, Mr. Right, and Being Your Whole You

Your Whole You Journal

Connect-

Email me at yourwholeyou@yahoo.com

Follow me on Instagram @yourwholeyoupublishing

Like me on Facebook @beyourwholeyou

Made in the USA
Columbia, SC
14 September 2023

22891648R00043